LIFESAVING SCIENCE

VACCINES

By Joanna Brundle

Enslow
PUBLISHING

Published in 2021 by Enslow Publishing, LLC
101 W. 23rd Street, Suite 240,
New York, NY 10011

© 2019 Booklife Publishing
This edition is published by arrangement with Booklife
Publishing

Cataloging-in-Publication Data

Names: Brundle, Joanna.
Title: Vaccines / Joanna Brundle.
Description: New York : Enslow Publishing, 2021. | Series:
Lifesaving science | Includes glossary and index.
Identifiers: ISBN 9781978519473 (pbk.) | ISBN 9781978519497
(library bound) | ISBN 9781978519480 (6 pack)
Subjects: LCSH: Vaccines--Juvenile literature. | Vaccination--
Juvenile literature.
Classification: LCC RA638.B78 2021 | DDC 615.3'72--dc23

Printed in the United States of America

CPSIA compliance information: Batch #BS20ENS: For further information contact
Enslow Publishing, New York, New York at 1-800-542-2595

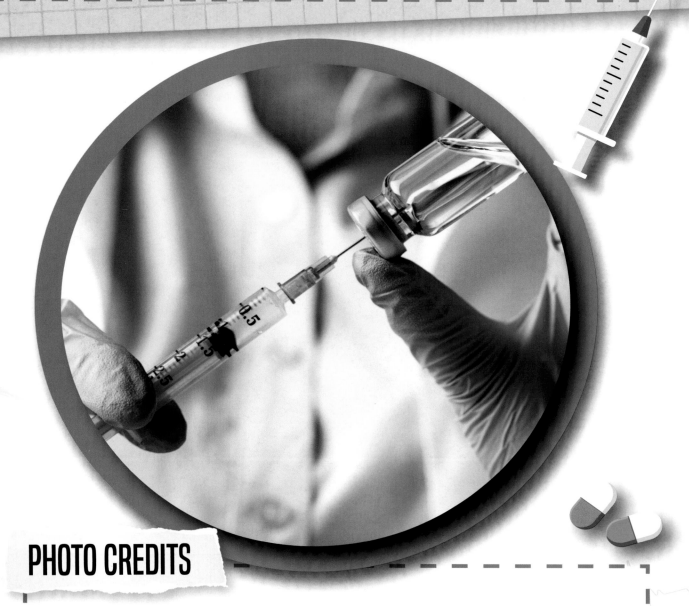

PHOTO CREDITS

Front Cover – Valeriya Anufriyeva, Sylfida, vector toon, StudioAz, Leone_V. 2 – Billion Photos. 4&5 – didesign021, vitstudio, John-Kelly. 6&7 – Designua, Barabasa, Dionisvera, Catalin Petolea, Africa Studio. 8&9 – Warren Price Photography, optimarc, nobeastsofierce, Alexey Godzenko, Phubes Juwattana. 10&11 – Meletios Verras, Tiplyashina Evgeniya, GOLFX. 12&13 – Everett Historical. 14&15 – Everett Historical, Georgios Kollidas. 16&17 – Everett Historical, Aksenova Natalya, nobeastsofierce, Victoria Antonova. 18&19 – RUCHUDA BOONPLIEN, Everett Historical, Kateryna Kon, gorillaimages. 20&21 – Guzsudio, Kateryna Kon, Everett Historical. 22&23 – Dzm1try, Robert Kneschke, Photographee.eu. 24&25 – rudram, ravipat, Africa Studio. 26&27 – Linda Bestwic, phichet chaiyabin, Chaikom, Jeffrey Paul Wade. 28&29 – Kilroy79, Gorodenkoff, StockSmartStart, Joa Souza, George Rudy. 30 – Artemida-psy, studiovin, moj0j0, KittyVector, Jamesbin, Sovenko Artem. Borders on all pages – Leone_V. Vectors throughout – Sylfida. Ripped paper throughout – BLACKDAY. Heart rate vector – StudioAz. Logo heart – vector toon. Images are courtesy of Shutterstock.com. With thanks to Getty Images, Thinkstock Photo and iStockphoto.

CONTENTS

Words that look like **THIS** can be found in the glossary on page **31.**

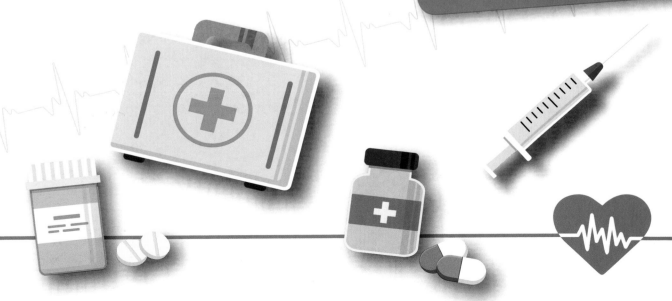

THE WORLD OF MEDICINE

Every day, millions of people around the world suffer from minor and serious illnesses and receive treatment for them. They may have become infected with a disease, had an accident, or been admitted to the hospital for routine or emergency treatment. They are looked after by **HEALTH-CARE PROFESSIONALS** who have been trained to give the care they need. Patients rely on these professionals and the treatments they give to return them to full health. Sometimes medical problems are life-threatening, but a huge range of lifesaving medicines and treatments are available to health-care professionals to help them to prevent, find, and treat medical problems. Vaccines are an example of this kind of lifesaving miracle.

VACCINATIONS CAN SAVE YOUR LIFE.

Polio is a disease that can lead to paralysis or death.

Since 1900, worldwide average life expectancy (the amount of time that a newborn baby is expected to live for) has more than doubled and is now over 70 years. Scientists are predicting that average life expectancy will eventually reach over 100 years in some societies. There are many reasons for this. Improved health care has been very important and vaccines have played a vital part. Their introduction has led to the prevention of many serious or deadly diseases. In many parts of the world, good health and health care are now accepted as normal parts of life, so it is easy to forget that this hasn't always been the case, and still isn't in some places. Diseases that can now be prevented easily and effectively by vaccines used to kill or permanently disable thousands of people every year. In this book, we will be taking a look at the discovery and development of vaccines and their lifesaving role in modern medicine.

CHICKENPOX RASH

WHAT ARE VACCINES?

Vaccines allow the body to have a trial run at fighting a disease, without the body actually being infected with the disease. A vaccine is a small amount of a safe version of the disease in a dead or weakened form. The vaccine is powerful enough to trick the body into thinking it has become infected, but not powerful enough to cause the symptoms of the disease.

FACT

DEAD FORM = INACTIVATED

WEAKENED FORM = ATTENUATED

THE INNATE IMMUNE SYSTEM

The immune system is made up of the **ORGANS** and processes of the body that give protection against diseases and toxins (poisons). Once an infection threatens the body, the immune system begins to defend the body in two stages. The innate immune system is the body's first line of defense. It is made up of physical barriers to disease, such as the skin and **MUCOUS MEMBRANES**, and **CELLS** that attack any **MICROBES** that have invaded the body. Phagocytes (say: FA-guh-sites) are white blood cells that wrap themselves around invaders, engulfing and destroying them. Natural killer cells are also white blood cells that kill invaders by injecting them with lethal toxins.

THE ADAPTIVE IMMUNE SYSTEM

The adaptive immune system is more complex and responds more slowly. Substances, called antigens, on the invading cells are identified and the body then produces an army of cells called antibodies. Antibodies are specifically designed – or adapted – to fight that particular antigen.

MEMORY CELLS

The first time the body comes into contact with a disease, it can take several days for the adaptive immune system to fight back. During that time, an illness, such as the whooping cough (say: hooping coff) virus may spread rapidly through the body and cause serious problems. The antibodies that the body produces eventually break down after the threat of the disease has passed, but some immune cells, called memory cells, remain in the body. If the body comes into contact with the same disease again, memory cells remember which antibody is needed to fight the disease. They then produce huge numbers of that antibody very quickly. By tricking the immune system into action, vaccines enable the body to produce memory cells, without the vaccinated person geting the disease itself. In the future, the body can fight back quickly against the same infection.

Whooping cough is also called pertussis, and is a **CONTAGIOUS** disease that causes severe coughing followed by a whooping sound as the patient breathes in.

YOU CAN HELP TO PROTECT YOUR IMMUNE SYSTEM BY EATING A HEALTHY, VARIED DIET, BY GETTING LOTS OF EXERCISE, AND BY GETTING ENOUGH SLEEP.

DISEASE AND HOW THE BODY RESPONDS

ANTIGENS

The human body is constantly in contact with **MICROSCOPIC** pathogens. These are tiny **ORGANISMS**, such as bacteria and viruses, that can cause disease if they enter the bloodstream or body tissues. Pathogens, which are often called "germs," are found everywhere, such as in food, water, soil, and air.

Although most diseases are caused by bacteria and viruses, some are caused by parasites and fungi. Diseases can be spread by coughs and sneezes, physical contact between people, and touching infected surfaces such as door handles and counters. Some diseases are carried in saliva and other body fluids.

Disease Checklist

Bacteria
- living single-celled organisms
- multiply by splitting into two new cells

Viruses
- nonliving **GENETIC MATERIAL** with a **PROTEIN** coating
- live inside host cells where they multiply by building copies of themselves

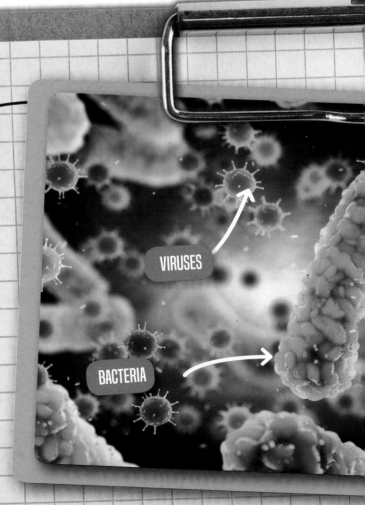

VIRUSES

BACTERIA

ANTIBODY

Each antibody recognizes and binds only to a particular antigen.

As we have seen, antigens are found on the surface of bacteria and viruses. Antigens prompt the body to produce antibodies. The term "antigen" is short for "antibody generators." Each antigen is different and each is attacked by a specific antibody. Antibodies – also known as immunoglobulins (say: im-yoo-noh-GLAHB-yoo-lihns) – are protective, Y-shaped proteins. Antibodies behave like sniffer dogs for the immune system, finding antigens and sticking to them. They are fitted with special **RECEPTORS** that bind only to a particular antigen – just as a puzzle piece clicks into the correct place and won't fit anywhere else. The part of an antigen to which an antibody attaches itself is called the epitope. The part of an antibody that recognizes and sticks to an antigen is called the paratope.

Parasites
– Live and feed on or in other organisms (hosts)

Parasitic worms can live in the human **INTESTINE** and cause disease.

Fungi
– Living organisms
– Can be large, for example toadstools, or microscopic, such as mold

Nail infections are caused by fungi.

T-CELLS AND B-CELLS

T-cells and B-cells are white blood cells that are part of the adaptive immune system and fight specific infections. T-cells are called this because they develop in a small organ called the thymus gland. B-cells are called this because they develop in **BONE MARROW**. If the body is invaded by a disease, only the T- and B-cells that are specific to that infection respond. Different T-cells have different jobs. Some destroy virus-infected cells directly. Some send chemical instructions, called cytokines, to the immune system. Other T-cells help B-cells to make antibodies. B-cells recognize the surface antigens of bacteria and viruses and spring into action as antibody factories. The antibodies they produce stick to the antigens to form clumps. The body recognizes these as invaders and marks them out for destruction. Some T- and B-cells are memory cells (see page 7). Each time the body is exposed to the same infection, they become better at fighting that infection.

FACT

A HEALTHY BODY MAY PRODUCE MILLIONS OF INFECTION-FIGHTING ANTIBODIES EVERY DAY, WITHOUT THE PERSON EVEN REALIZING THAT THEY HAVE BEEN EXPOSED TO AN ANTIGEN.

INNATE (NATURAL) IMMUNITY IN BABIES

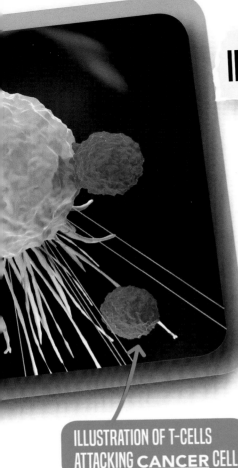

ILLUSTRATION OF T-CELLS ATTACKING **CANCER** CELL

Babies are born with natural **IMMUNITY** to some diseases. It is a built-in defense system. This means that it doesn't have to be learned by being exposed to a disease. During the last three months of pregnancy, antibodies from the mother are passed through the **PLACENTA** to her unborn child. The types and amounts of antibodies that are passed on depend on the mother's immunity. If, for example, she has had chickenpox (varicella), she will have developed immunity to it and will pass chickenpox antibodies to her baby. After a few weeks, the immunity of newborn babies starts to decrease, so infants begin a series of vaccinations against many diseases, usually from the age of about two months. The immunity that newborn babies have is called passive immunity, because they have been given the antibodies, rather than making them for themselves.

Breast milk contains antibodies, so breastfed babies keep their passive immunity for longer than bottle-fed babies.

ALLERGIES

The body's immune system can mistakenly identify things that are harmless to most people as harmful invaders. Animal fur or pollen, for example, can produce an allergic reaction, such as a rash. Anaphylaxis is a rare but very serious allergic reaction that can be fatal.

THE HISTORY OF VACCINES

As long ago as 429 BC, the Greek historian Thucydides noticed that patients who recovered from smallpox seemed to be protected from catching the same disease again. He had no idea why this was so, but had identified that the body's immune system was kicking into action.

VARIOLATION

Many centuries later, the practice of variolation (say: va-ree-oh-LAY-shun) appeared in Asia. Dried, crushed-up scabs from a patient infected with smallpox were blown directly into the nose of another person. This person then contracted a mild form of the disease, but recovered from it and was also immune to future infection. By 1700, variolation had spread to India, Africa, and Southeastern Europe.

SMALLPOX

Smallpox caused pain, fever, and a rash of spots containing pus. Around a third of sufferers died from the disease. Those who recovered were badly scarred. Many were left blind or brain-damaged. The disease was thought to have been in existence for over 12,000 years, and during that time it killed and harmed millions of people.

Smallpox was caused by the variola virus.

FACT

THE FIRST IDENTIFIED VICTIM OF SMALLPOX IS THE EGYPTIAN PHARAOH RAMSES V, WHO IS THOUGHT TO HAVE DIED FROM THE DISEASE IN 1157 BC. SPOTS THAT LOOK LIKE SMALLPOX SCARS CAN BE SEEN ON HIS MUMMIFIED BODY.

SCARRING CAUSED BY SMALLPOX

LADY MARY WORTLEY MONTAGU

In 1717, Lady Mary Wortley Montagu heard about variolation in Constantinople (modern-day Istanbul, Turkey). She had suffered from smallpox herself and wanted to help other people. In England, in 1721, she was responsible for a number of prisoners and abandoned children being variolated by having smallpox scabs scratched into their skin. A few months later, the same people were deliberately exposed to smallpox again. None of them caught the disease because they had developed immunity to it. Members of the English royal family were variolated and the practice became fashionable across Europe.

FACT

VARIOLATION WAS QUITE RISKY, KILLING AROUND ONE IN 50 VARIOLATED PEOPLE. BUT, SMALLPOX ITSELF KILLED 15 OUT OF EVERY 50 PEOPLE WHO BECAME INFECTED.

SMALLPOX VACCINATIONS, NEW YORK CITY, 1872

VARIOLATION IN THE U.S.

Variolation was introduced to the United States by African slaves. Cotton Mather was told about the practice by his slave, Onesimus. He spread the word and variolation was tested out during a smallpox **EPIDEMIC** that hit Boston, Massachusetts, in 1721.

EDWARD JENNER

In 1796, a British doctor, Edward Jenner (1749–1823), discovered a safer method than variolation. He had noticed that during a smallpox outbreak, milkmaids rarely caught the disease. They did, however, often catch cowpox, a disease caught by touching the udders of infected cows. Cowpox caused unsightly pustules but was not dangerous. Jenner realized that having cowpox somehow protected the milkmaids from smallpox. He collected pus from the cowpox pustules on the hands and arms of a young milkmaid, Sarah Nelmes. On May 14, 1796, he scratched it into the skin of an eight-year-old boy, James Phipps. A single pustule appeared on the boy's skin, but he quickly recovered. On July 1, 1796, Jenner repeated the procedure on the same boy, but this time using smallpox pus. The boy remained well, suggesting that **INOCULATING** him with cowpox had made him immune to smallpox.

THE VACCINATION OF JAMES PHIPPS

FACT

IT MAY BE THAT ENGLISH FARMER BENJAMIN JESTY WAS, IN FACT, THE FIRST PERSON TO INOCULATE AGAINST SMALLPOX USING COWPOX. DURING A SMALLPOX EPIDEMIC IN 1774, JESTY INOCULATED HIS WIFE AND CHILDREN WITH COWPOX, BUT HE DIDN'T TELL ANYONE AND JENNER WAS CREDITED WITH THE DISCOVERY.

EDWARD JENNER

In 1797, Jenner presented his findings to the Royal Society of London, a group of leading scientists. They dismissed Jenner's ideas, saying that they were unproven and were too revolutionary. Jenner, however, knew he was on to something and continued his tests on other children. He even inoculated his own baby son. Finally, in 1798, his work was published. Jenner came up with the term "vaccination," from the Latin word *vacca*, meaning "cow." At first, people made fun of Jenner. He was particularly criticized by religious groups. They claimed that the practice of inoculating a person with something that originally came from a diseased animal was disgusting and ungodly. In 1802, a famous cartoon appeared that showed people who had been vaccinated growing cows' heads. But gradually, the evidence of the effectiveness of vaccines grew and their use became widespread. Jenner became a celebrity and spent much of the rest of his life **RESEARCHING** vaccines. His discovery of vaccination has saved millions of lives.

LOUIS PASTEUR

Almost a century later, the story moved to France. In 1877, scientist Louis Pasteur (1822–1895) was studying a disease called chicken cholera (say: CAH-luh-ruh). He reasoned that if Jenner had found a vaccine against smallpox, it must be possible to find a vaccine against chicken cholera – and all other diseases. In 1879, he made a startling, chance discovery.

Louis Pasteur was the first to prepare a vaccine in the laboratory.

In recognition of Pasteur's work, the bacterium that causes chicken cholera is called *Pasteurella*.

PASTEUR'S DISCOVERY

Having identified the bacteria that caused chicken cholera, Pasteur instructed his assistant to inject **LABORATORY** chickens with fresh **CULTURES** of the bacteria. The absentminded assistant forgot and did not inject the chickens until he realized his error, a month later. Instead of developing cholera, the chickens became only mildly infected and survived. Fascinated by this unexpected turn of events, Pasteur reinjected the same chickens. This time, he used fresh cultures of the bacteria, expecting the chickens to become sick and die. Instead, the disease had no effect. Pasteur realized that the first set of bacteria cultures had been weakened by exposure to **OXYGEN** in the air. He had accidentally discovered the attenuated – or weakened – vaccine.

FACT

CHOLERA IS A BACTERIAL DISEASE THAT CAUSES VOMITING, DIARRHEA, AND, OFTEN DEATH.

ANTHRAX

In 1879, Pasteur began investigating **ANTHRAX**, an epidemic that was killing many sheep as well as humans. Together with German scientist Robert Koch (1843–1910), Pasteur isolated the bacterium causing the disease, *Bacillus anthracis*. He worked out how to produce a weakened version of the disease and, in 1881, began vaccination experiments on sheep. The vaccine was a success – all the vaccinated sheep were unaffected when injected with the disease itself.

FACT

PASTEUR'S VACCINES WERE FIRST CALLED "PASTEUR'S TREATMENT," BUT HE DECIDED TO GIVE THEM ALL THE NAME "VACCINES," TO RECOGNIZE THE WORK OF EDWARD JENNER.

RABIES AND RABBITS

In 1885, while studying **RABIES**, Pasteur produced his first human vaccine. Rabies had puzzled Pasteur because he could not find the microorganism causing it. Unknown to Pasteur, rabies is caused by a virus. Viruses multiply and mutate (change) quickly. Pasteur passed the virus through rabbits, causing it to mutate and become less dangerous to humans. He collected the mutated form from the rabbits' **SPINAL CORDS** and prepared his attenuated rabies vaccine. Pasteur first used the vaccine to protect dogs against rabies. He then injected a nine-year-old boy who had been attacked by wild, rabid dogs, but who had not yet developed rabies. The boy never developed rabies – the vaccine had worked.

Wild dogs may carry rabies and pass it on to humans if they bite them.

POLIO

Polio is an infectious, viral disease. It attacks the nervous system and can be serious, causing permanent paralysis or even death. The first reported epidemic occurred in the United States in 1894 and was followed by regular, serious outbreaks until the discovery of a vaccine in the 1950s.

Polio survivors often wore metal leg callipers to support muscles weakened by the disease.

JONAS SALK

American scientist Jonas Salk (1914–1995) discovered and produced the first polio vaccine. Using **FORMALDEHYDE**, Salk killed the polio virus but ensured that it was still able to trigger the body's immune system. The biggest **CLINICAL TRIALS** in the history of the United States were carried out in 1954 and a successful nationwide vaccination program began in 1955. Recorded cases of polio dropped from 58,000 in 1952 to 5,600 in 1957.

Polio can affect muscles used in breathing. The iron lung, a metal tank with a pump, was used to help affected patients.

ALBERT SABIN

Another scientist, Albert Sabin (1906–1993), developed a weakened form of the live virus. He experimented on monkeys and chimps and produced a vaccine that people could swallow. It was licensed for use in 1962 and quickly replaced the Salk vaccine because it was easy to take and provided longer-lasting immunity. Polio cases in the United States fell to 121 in 1964.

DIPHTHERIA

Diphtheria is a serious bacterial infection that is very contagious. It was once a major cause of illness and death in children. In 1921, there were 206,000 cases in the United States alone. The bacteria that cause diphtheria produce a toxin that kills off cells in the mouth, throat, and nose. The dead cells build up and form a membrane that can block the throat, leading to death by choking. In the 1890s, German doctor Emil von Behring (1854–1917) developed an antitoxin that neutralized the toxin. The first successful vaccine was developed in 1913 and gradually became widely used. The diphtheria vaccine is a toxoid – a toxin modified with heat and chemicals. The toxoid cannot produce the disease but prompts the body to produce antibodies. Although diphtheria is rare in industrialized countries like the United States, it is still common in Asia, the South Pacific, the Middle East, Eastern Europe, and the Caribbean.

ILLUSTRATION OF THE DIPHTHERIA BACTERIUM, *CORYNEBACTERIUM DIPHTHERIAE*

Diphtheria vaccines are usually combined with vaccines against TETANUS and whooping cough.

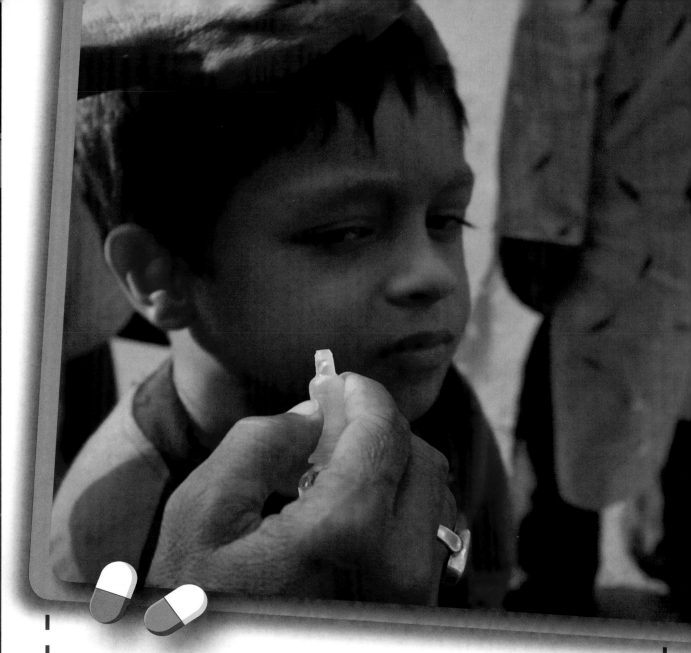

Vaccination gradually became widespread across the world as vaccines were produced against many of the world's most deadly diseases. By the end of the 1920s, effective vaccinations were available for diphtheria, tetanus, whooping cough, and **TUBERCULOSIS**. During the 1960s, vaccinations became available for **MEASLES** (1963), **MUMPS** (1967), and **RUBELLA** (1969). These were combined into a single vaccination called MMR in 1971. In 1956, the **WORLD HEALTH ORGANIZATION** (WHO) began efforts to vaccinate people worldwide against smallpox. As a result, the disease was declared to have been eradicated (wiped out) from the world in 1980. Polio is also now extremely rare and is very close to being eradicated. Since 1988, polio cases have dropped by over 99% from 350,000 cases then worldwide, to just 22 cases in 2017, mainly in Nigeria, Afghanistan, and Pakistan. In the last 30 years, many further vaccines have been introduced against diseases such as chickenpox (1996) and **SHINGLES** (2008).

CERVICAL CANCER

Cervical cancer is a serious disease that affects women. Professor Harald zur Hausen discovered that cervical cancer is often caused by viruses belonging to a group called human papillomavirus (HPV). His work led to the introduction in 2006 of a vaccine against HPV, which is now widely used to vaccinate teenage girls. This is the first time that a routine vaccine that is available to everyone has been used to guard against a type of cancer.

ILLUSTRATION OF HUMAN PAPILLOMAVIRUS

INFLUENZA

A U.S. ARMY HOSPITAL INFLUENZA WARD IN 1918

Influenza, often called the flu, is a contagious disease caused by viruses. It can be very serious, even deadly. Flu viruses can mutate rapidly, which means that the antigens are not recognized by the antibodies we already have in our bodies. Flu vaccines have been available since the 1940s, but because the virus keeps changing, scientists have to produce different vaccines each year. In 1918, a new type of flu, called Spanish flu, appeared. No vaccine was available and Spanish flu infected 500 million people worldwide.

FACT

AROUND 50 MILLION PEOPLE DIED IN THE SPANISH FLU **PANDEMIC**, MORE THAN WERE KILLED THROUGHOUT WORLD WAR I.

HERD IMMUNITY

Vaccinating the majority of people in a population creates herd immunity. Herd immunity means resistance to the spread of infection within a population. It comes about when a high proportion of individuals in that population are immune to the disease, thanks to vaccination. Anyone who has not been vaccinated is very unlikely to come into contact with someone with the disease. The disease is therefore prevented from spreading and dies out. Herd immunity protects both the majority of people who have been vaccinated and also the few who have not been vaccinated. The more contagious a disease is, the more people need to be vaccinated for herd immunity to work. This diagram shows how it works.

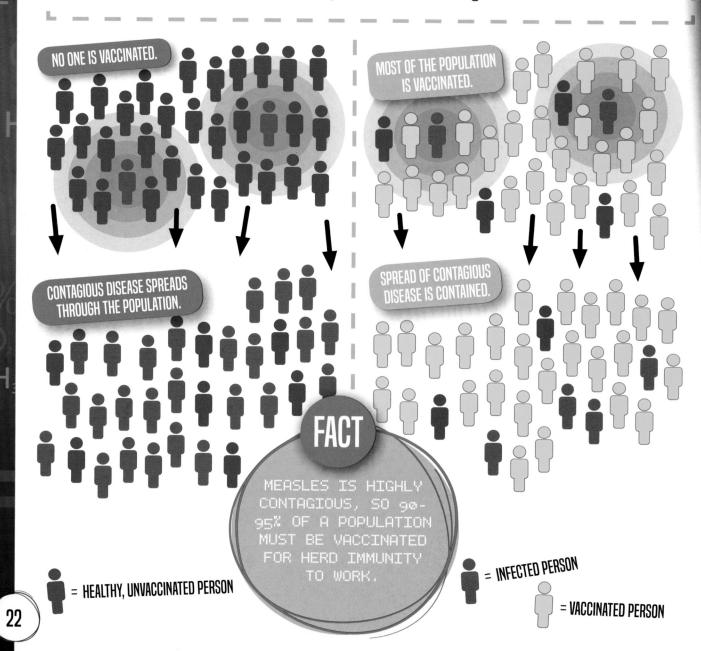

NO ONE IS VACCINATED.

MOST OF THE POPULATION IS VACCINATED.

CONTAGIOUS DISEASE SPREADS THROUGH THE POPULATION.

SPREAD OF CONTAGIOUS DISEASE IS CONTAINED.

FACT

MEASLES IS HIGHLY CONTAGIOUS, SO 90-95% OF A POPULATION MUST BE VACCINATED FOR HERD IMMUNITY TO WORK.

= HEALTHY, UNVACCINATED PERSON

= INFECTED PERSON

= VACCINATED PERSON

Herd immunity relies on everyone who can be vaccinated doing so. But there are some people who cannot be vaccinated, including very young babies, elderly or sick people, and those whose immune system has been weakened. This weakness might be due to illnesses such as **AIDS** or cancers of the immune system. People who have previously had an allergic reaction to a vaccine or who are allergic to any of the ingredients in the vaccine should not be vaccinated. People who cannot be vaccinated are still protected by herd immunity.

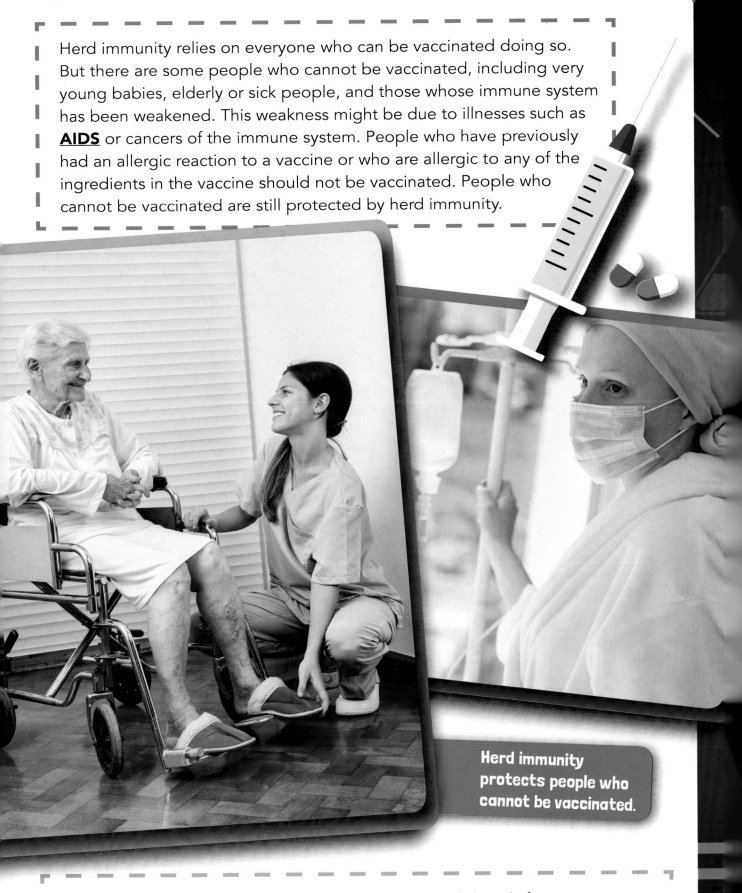

Herd immunity protects people who cannot be vaccinated.

Herd immunity only works for diseases that are passed directly from one person to another. It would not work, for example, against tetanus, which is caused by a bacterium in soil. Anyone who has not been vaccinated but comes into contact with the bacterium, for example by getting dirt in a cut on their hand, might get the disease, even if everyone around them has been vaccinated.

HAVING A VACCINATION

Vaccines can be given:

- By injection using a hypodermic syringe.

- Directly into the mouth (used for vaccines against diseases such as cholera that are carried in food and water and enter the body through the mouth).

- Using a nasal spray (used for some flu vaccines).

Before a vaccination injection is given, the area is cleaned using a disinfectant swab.

A hypodermic needle has a pointed end that pierces skin easily. It is hollow, to allow the vaccine to be pushed into the body when the syringe plunger is pushed.

Having an injection sounds scary, but you only feel a small, sharp scratch – a small price to pay for protection from horrible diseases. Vaccines are very safe and have to go through strict testing to ensure their safety and effectiveness before they can be licensed for use on the public. For many diseases, several doses of the vaccine are needed to build up full, long-lasting immunity. It is very important to keep your vaccinations up to date and to go for booster injections when necessary. Most people feel fine after a vaccination, but some feel sick or have soreness where the injection was given for a short time. Very occasionally, a person may have a severe allergic reaction called anaphylaxis after a vaccination (see page 11), although this is rare.

FACT

IF YOU FEEL UNWELL BEFORE A VACCINATION, IT IS BETTER TO WAIT UNTIL YOU FEEL BETTER BEFORE BEING VACCINATED.

FOREIGN TRAVEL

If you travel abroad, you may need to have extra vaccinations, especially if you are visiting tropical countries. These vaccinations protect you from diseases that you might be exposed to, such as cholera or **TYPHOID**. Your parent or caregiver should always check which vaccinations are required or recommended for the countries you are visiting before you travel. Always allow enough time to receive the correct number of doses and for immunity to build up before you travel.

Visitors to South Africa's national parks are advised to have vaccinations against typhoid, cholera, **YELLOW FEVER**, rabies, **HEPATITIS A AND B**, and influenza.

VACCINES IN LESS ECONOMICALLY DEVELOPED COUNTRIES (LEDCs)

Vaccines are expensive to develop and produce. In less economically developed countries (LEDCs), mass vaccination programs may be funded and organized by charities and by organizations such as the WHO. Vaccination programs in LEDCs help some of the world's poorest people to lead healthier, happier lives.

Dogs can be vaccinated against kennel cough, which can spread rapidly in boarding kennels where dogs are in close contact with one another.

FACT

FARM AND ZOO ANIMALS AND DOMESTIC PETS CAN ALSO BE VACCINATED TO PREVENT THE SPREAD OF DISEASE. MANY BOARDING KENNELS ASK TO SEE VACCINATION CERTIFICATES BEFORE PETS ARE ALLOWED TO STAY.

VACCINE-PREVENTABLE DISEASES

A vaccine-preventable disease is a disease for which an effective vaccine exists. Deaths from these diseases are called vaccine-preventable deaths. There are now over 25 vaccine-preventable diseases. In addition to those we have already looked at, vaccine-preventable diseases include meningitis. Meningitis attacks the protective membranes covering the brain and spinal cord. Unless it is treated quickly, meningitis can lead to fatal **SEPTICEMIA** (say: sehp-tih-SEE-me-ah) or permanent brain or nerve damage. It can be caused by bacterial or viral infections. Vaccinations provide protection against some of the causes of meningitis.

A rash that does not disappear when a glass is rolled over it is a common sign of septicemia.

FACT

SYMPTOMS OF MENINGITIS INCLUDE FEVER, VOMITING, HEADACHE, A STIFF NECK, AND A DISLIKE OF BRIGHT LIGHTS. IF YOU OR A FRIEND HAVE THESE SYMPTOMS, EVEN IF THERE IS NO RASH, ACT FAST. TELL AN ADULT RIGHT AWAY.

MEASLES RASH

Each year, over 100 million children worldwide are now vaccinated against some preventable diseases. Despite this success, however, around 3 million people around the world die every year from vaccine-preventable diseases. Of these, an estimated 1.5 million are children under five. Between 2000 and 2016, the safe and cost-effective measles vaccine saved around 20 million lives, but each year, thousands of unvaccinated people, mostly children under five, still die from this vaccine-preventable disease.

Measles can lead to death or serious complications including permanent hearing loss.

NON-VACCINE-PREVENTABLE DISEASES

Ebola is an example of a disease for which an effective vaccine is not yet available. The Ebola virus was first discovered in 1976 near the Ebola River in an African country now known as the Democratic Republic of Congo. The largest known outbreak occurred in 2014–2015 across Guinea, Liberia, and Sierra Leone. WHO reported 28,000 cases, with 11,000 deaths. Further outbreaks occurred in the Congo in 2017 and 2018. Scientists are working on possible new vaccines, which are currently being tested. Ring vaccination, using these experimental vaccines, involves vaccinating the "ring" of people who have been in contact with someone who has the virus, for example their family members and friends.

Doctors and nurses treating Ebola patients have to wear protective clothing because the disease is very contagious and is spread in blood and other body fluids.

NIPAH VIRUS DISEASE

Nipah virus causes symptoms that are often deadly and include fever, breathing problems, and swelling of the brain. Like Ebola, Nipah is a zoonotic disease, which means it is passed to humans from animals, including fruit bats. Occasionally, it spreads between humans, and scientists are racing to find an effective vaccine before the virus mutates enough to be able to spread easily and rapidly between people.

Nipah virus is carried by fruit bats and is spread to humans when they eat fruit contaminated with body fluids from infected bats.

VACCINATIONS IN THE FUTURE

NEW VACCINATION METHODS

In the future, injections might be replaced with other methods of giving vaccinations, such as stick-on patches with very fine needles you can hardly feel. This might be useful in remote places with limited health care because, unlike injections, patches don't have to be given by trained health-care professionals. Scientists are also researching vaccines you can eat, produced in the edible parts of **GENETICALLY MODIFIED PLANTS**, including bananas and tomatoes.

VACCINATION PROBLEMS IN LEDCs

There are still parts of the world where vaccinating people is difficult. This may be because of wars, **NATURAL DISASTERS**, or the high costs involved. In order to work, some vaccines have to be stored at low temperatures. Temperature-controlled storage and the electricity needed to run it are often not available in parts of the world where vaccines are most needed. Research is continuing into producing vaccines that can be made more cheaply, stored at any temperature, and that remain effective even if stored for long periods.

Developing a new vaccine typically takes 10 years.